YOUNG

Entrepreneurs

The stories of eight successful young entrepreneurs, how they became successful and what you can do to be just as successful as they are

Samuel Dixon

inattention, use or misuse of the information in question by the reader will render any resulting actions solely under their purview. There are no scenarios in which the publisher or the original author of this work can be in any fashion deemed liable for any hardship or damages that may befall them after undertaking information described herein.

Additionally, the information in the following pages is intended only for informational purposes and should thus be thought of as universal. As befitting its nature, it is presented without assurance regarding its prolonged validity or interim quality. Trademarks that are mentioned are done without written consent and can in no way be considered an endorsement from the trademark holder.

Table of Contents

Introduction

Congratulations on purchasing this book and thank you for doing so.

The following chapters will give you information about the most successful young entrepreneurs, how they got to the point they are at today and how you can do it, too. There are various strategies that you can use to help you learn how to be a great entrepreneur.

There are plenty of books on this subject on the market, thanks again for choosing this one! Every effort was made to ensure it is full of as much useful information as possible, please enjoy!

Chapter 1: The Basics of Entrepreneurship

Before you can learn about the young, successful entrepreneurs of the world and begin your *own* journey to success, you should have some basic knowledge of what it means to be an entrepreneur and what it means to be a successful one. While there are millions of people around the world who are working to become successful, there are a few key things that set them apart from the true entrepreneurs.

Definition of Entrepreneur

Someone who is an entrepreneur is a person who is able to create a business or several businesses and operate them. They are a mixture between a businessperson and an inventor. They come up with great ideas for businesses, and they want to make sure that they are successful above all else. They have great ideas, the power to secure them and, most importantly, the capital that is required to start a successful business (and continue to fund it).

An entrepreneur is someone who is able to try new things and influence others to do the same. Someone who exhibits entrepreneur-like behavior is able to create a lot of different things and opportunities for other people. They work to help people learn how to do more and have more and they, above all, always try their hardest to be successful.

Being an entrepreneur does not require someone to go to school, learn different things or try to be one. It is a character trait that some people just have, and they are able to use it for their own benefits. You can't necessarily learn to be an entrepreneur, but you can learn the things that will allow you to be successful and function as an entrepreneur.

If you have high aspirations for "something more," dreams that may seem impossible and the ability to come up with great ideas, the chances are that you are an entrepreneur.

What it Takes to be Successful

The number one thing that most successful entrepreneurs say that they have is a drive to do better and do more. They want to be able to always succeed, and they will stop at nothing to get to the point where they want to be. They work very hard with the different things that they can do, and they always want to make sure that they are successful.

Even when entrepreneurs are not doing well with the different things that they are working on doing, they still continue to push on. They do not let anything get in the way of their drive.

Along with a drive to do better and be better, they also have perseverance and the ability to continue trying. They are resilient, and they work hard to be able to get what they want. Entrepreneurs are usually very far from lazy, and that makes a difference when they are doing different things with their business. It is hard to change these characteristics and entrepreneurs are either born with them, or they are not able to use them to their benefit when it comes to different things.

Why Young People Usually Aren't

The majority of young people are still learning who they are, what they are good at and how they can be successful. For this reason, they are usually not entrepreneurs when it comes to the way that they do things. It is hard to be a true entrepreneur when you are still learning who you are and what you are capable of. The small number of people who are able to be successful as entrepreneurs at a young age are the people who are able to get the most out of different situations. These people usually see success very young and are able to tell that they are going to be great at what they do from early on.

The Risks of Entrepreneurship

Many entrepreneurial opportunities require people to put up a lot of money, put in a lot of time or make a lot of different commitments. These are all risks that are associated with different entrepreneurial positions, and it is important that people realize this when they are getting started with being entrepreneurs. Whether they are putting up time, money or anything else all depends on the type of business that they are going to start and this can be different in different industries. Entrepreneurs, though, usually recognize the risks that are associated with their business and they see that the success of the business will be worth far more than the risks that they take.

By definition, entrepreneurship is a risk. It is something that people will need to consider when they want to start a business or businesses. It is also something that will need to be factored in when looking at the profits and the payoffs that come from being an entrepreneur.

Different from the All of the Others

Most of the people who are entrepreneurs can recognize from early on that they are different from other people. Whether they notice that they are more driven, have a better attitude or work harder than others all depends on their personality. It is important to note that entrepreneurs all have a different mindset than other people and it is something that they need to discuss when they are doing different things. Entrepreneurs are different from the rest, and their success is often because they are a different type of person than others who do things the "normal" way or who are content with just being where they are at in life instead of becoming more successful.

Chapter 2: Brian Chesky

Young Entrepreneurs

As the founder of the increasingly popular Airbnb, Brian Chesky first became a successful entrepreneur when he was just under 30 years old. He has been able to overcome struggles, has gone through various steps and now has a very successful business that is growing by the day. He works hard to make sure that he is doing everything the right way and this allows him the chance to make sure that he can do more with the business that he has. He wants to make sure that he works hard and this gives him the chance to keep ground his business.

Before the Fortune

Not unlike many of the other entrepreneurs who are included on this list, Brian Chesky was able to go to college and get the degree that he wanted. Working as an engineer, he was able to see that there were many aspects of life that he wanted to be different. While he *was* successful in the career that he had, he also knew that there was more to life than just working a normal job.

After graduating from college, he moved to San Francisco where he continued his industrialized career. He worked very hard, and he actually had a roommate to help him save money. He later found that having a roommate would be a blessing because it would allow him the chance to continue on with his career and to build a business that is much more successful than he would have ever been in the industrial sector that he had originally set out to be a part of.

Inspiration

While Chesky was working as an engineer and living with a roommate, there was a convention where there were a lot of people coming to. They were all engineers just like he was and he and his roommate offered up their apartment for the people to stay in while they were there for the convention.

Having all of these houseguests who were staying with him for nothing allowed Brian to get inspiration on something he had never even considered in the past. He thought it would be a great idea to rent out his apartment for a short period of time to people who needed a place to stay. Almost similar to bed and breakfast but different in the fact that they would be sharing the place where the person lived instead of trying to make it exclusive for guests. This is where Airbnb was born and where it continues to grow from.

Brian, in combination with his roommate and now business partner, started thinking of the different things that he could do to grow this into a business. He wanted to be able to rent out his own apartment, but he also wanted others to have the chance to do so, too. This is where the website for Airbnb came in and, subsequently, the app that so many people now use today to be able to book a stay at someone's house.

Airbnb is less expensive than traditional accommodations, allows guests to feel like they are getting the authentic experience and creates a sense of community. It also helps to generate income in an entirely new way for the people who are renting out their space to the guests who are coming from different destinations. Airbnb has been so successful because Chesky had a great idea and never gave up on it.

Worth

Brian Chesky is able to be much more comfortable than he ever would have been as an engineer. While that market is lucrative, it turns out that running your own service with an app and website included is even more lucrative.

Brian Chesky, who is under 40 years old, is worth 3.3 billion United States dollars. This may seem like a lot, but it is a number that has steadily risen since Chesky first started Airbnb. He was successful at the beginning, but he has been even more successful since that time. It is expected that he will be worth over 5 billion dollars by the time he is 45 years old as long as Airbnb continues to flourish.

Growing Market

The hospitality industry has changed so much since Airbnb was first started. It has been able to keep up with the different trends, and this has allowed it to be even better than what it once was. Technology has heavily influenced nearly every industry, but this is especially true with hospitality. People can now book a stay in a great house nearly anywhere in the world with the click of a button on an app that is right in the palm of their hands.

Technology is not expected to slow down anytime soon, and that is a great thing for hospitality. The industry is going to grow even more than what it already has. Right now, Airbnb has people who are constantly trying to take its spot as the number one in the industry, but it has been hard for them because Airbnb was the first and they continue to be the best. With all of the competition, Airbnb has seen more success than it ever thought possible but it still remains at the top of the list for the success of the business and the people who run it. None of the other, more obscure bed and breakfast applications have a CEO who is worth over 3 billion dollars.

Struggles with Airbnb

Since it was first introduced, regulators and other downers have been fighting for Airbnb to go away. This is because the big name hotels who previously had no major competition are actually seeing problems now. Brian Chesky was able to shake up the hospitality system, and many people did not like that. Despite the fact that there are new regulations and constant issues that arise, Chesky has been able to overcome all of that. His drive has allowed him to continue pushing forward and making Airbnb something that is so much more than a quick stay at a random person's house.

Chapter 3: Mark Zuckerberg

The chances are that you have heard of Mark Zuckerberg. He is popular in the world of entrepreneurship, he has a very successful business, and he even now has a movie that was created by his success. Even if you haven't heard of Zuckerberg, the chances are very high that you have heard of his business. Facebook is the worldwide phenomena of social media that have taken everyone by storm, has become a mega player in social media and has continued to flourish even when other social media sites are falling off of the face of the Internet.

Success Before Graduation

While the majority of people who are on this list have, in fact, graduated college by the time that they are successful, Mark Zuckerberg is different. He did graduation from college – Harvard, one of the best in the country – but he saw a lot of success before he even graduated. This was something that set him apart from many others and allowed him to be one of the youngest people who was successful at that time.

The success that he saw did not come in the form of tons of money or even in an extravagant lifestyle but it came in the form of having many people sign up for his site, and this gave him the reach that he needed to get to other people. He wanted to make sure that he was getting the most out of the experience and that he was able to show people that he was great at what he did. He also just wanted a chance for people to connect on a different level.

Computer Programming

While Zuckerberg was at Harvard, he was studying to become a computer programmer. He worked on many different platforms, but he knew that something had to be done about the social aspect of computers. Before Facebook was created, the only chance people had for communication was emailed that were not really convenient and sketchy chat rooms where they could be talking to anyone. He wanted to make it different and allow people to put a face to the others that they were talking to. This is where the idea for Facebook came about and it grew from that point to where it is today. Facebook was a phenomenal solution to a problem most people didn't even realize that they had.

When Facebook was first started, it was intended only for people to connect on the Harvard campus. They had to have a Harvard email address to do it, and that allowed them to connect with others.

Zuckerberg saw how great this would be and expanded it to other Ivy League schools. He then saw that people were still loving it just the same and expanded, yet again, to include anyone with a .edu email address. After seeing how people responded to it, he eventually opened it up to *anyone* who had an email address. That is when it truly started to take off and make a difference for people who wanted to have social media to communicate with others with.

Controversy Surrounding Zuck

While Facebook has been mostly smiling faces and rebuilding missed connections with high school best friends for the people who use it, it has not always been that way for the people who are running the site. The infamous battle between Zuckerberg and the other co-founders was actually well played out on the news and even made its appearance in the movie about the beginnings of Facebook, but it was nothing more than some controversy that Mark Zuckerberg had to get through.

Because of his entrepreneurial spirit, Zuckerberg wouldn't even let court cases, settlements, and harsh accusations bring him down when it came to being successful with Facebook. While he has not let on that anything has bothered him about the site and the subsequent controversy that surrounded it, it was sure to have been a problematic experience. Despite all of that, Facebook has continued to grow and so has Zuckerberg's insane net worth that keeps getting bigger and bigger.

Worth and Salary

It is often easy to see the success of an entrepreneur right in their net worth. This is something that many people describe as the single identification factor for the various problems that come along with being an entrepreneur. Even a business that has been successful may have a CEO who does not have a high net worth. This is not the case with Zuckerberg.

He is worth a cool 53.6 billion dollars for his work with Facebook and the way that he runs the business.

There is a big difference, though, of his worth and his salary. Unlike many CEOs of companies who are in it for the money, that has never been the case with Zuckerberg. He enjoys his own net worth and takes that into account instead of worrying about what he is going to do with his money that he can make from the business now. It is evidenced by the fact that he takes a 1 dollar per year salary and only takes that much because he *has* to have some type of salary to be considered the acting CEO of the company. This is something that makes a huge difference for the company and shows that Zuckerberg really just cares about Facebook and not the money.

The Face of Facebook

Even though you may be more familiar with the Facebook logo, the chances are that you have seen Zuckerberg's face at some point. While he doesn't make you be his "friend" like one other, previous social media site (that wasn't quite so successful), you can find Zuckerberg on Facebook. He has chosen to make all of the people who are on the site the face of it instead of making it all about himself. This is just another reason that shows that he is truly dedicated to Facebook.

One thing that sets Zuckerberg apart from the other entrepreneurs on this list is that, while he does run Facebook, he has taken a step back from the life of the rich and fabulous. He lives a simple life, does not frivolously spend his money and wants to focus his life more on his abilities than on the money that he has made in the past. It truly shows where his heart is in the business and that he is one of the best types of entrepreneurs out there. He knows that money will always follow success and his net worth is reflective of that belief.

Chapter 4: Jack Dorsey

Yet another social media mogul, Jack Dorsey was under 35 years old when he launched not his first, but his second, technology-based business that would eventually grow into a multimillion dollar operation and a name throughout households and small businesses around the world.

Fun fact: both Twitter and Square (two completely different technology-based businesses that are huge in their respective industries) share a co-founder. Can you guess who it is?

If you guessed Jack Dorsey, you are spot on.

A New Social Media

With the Facebooks and MySpaces of the world, Jack Dorsey (who is truly an artistic visionary) recognized the need for something simpler in the world of social media. He thought that it was great that people could spill their guts in posts that were hundreds of words long but he also knew that others were moving at the speed of light and they wanted to see only short blurbs. The idea behind this was that people could post more often and with more meaning if they only had a short amount of space to post what they had.

Thus, the character counted Twitter was born in the idea that people could share more meaningful updates about their lives more often if they were not trying to put together long, drawn out posts. Twitter grew from a simple idea that was based on instant messaging and other platforms to the giant that it is today. It has been successful in the time that it has been around but it has not been without tribulations.

Solutions for Businesses

While Jack was working with Twitter to grow it to something better, he recognized that there were other needs in the technology industry. Being a college dropout, he wanted to make sure that he was able to earn money somehow and he thought of another major genius solution that would help small businesses in a way that would not have ever been able to be done with the old style credit card machines.

Square was intended for people who wanted to be able to take credit cards but did not want to have to purchase the pricey machines to be able to do so. All they needed to do was add a bank account, link their Square up to it and plug a small device into their smartphone or their tablet. This is where they would swipe cards, and a small percentage would be given to the company for each of the things that they were able to do and for each of the charges that they had. It exploded into a huge industry, and other companies have been trying to copy it since it was first introduced in 2010. It was something that nobody could have predicted but also something that has continued to grow and become a huge business.

Not for Earning

While Square is something that has been making a lot of money because of the way that it operates, Twitter is the opposite. It was not designed or optimized to make money for people, and this was something that they knew they needed to do. While Facebook allows businesses and people to create advertisements, there were many problems that came along with doing the same thing on Twitter. This has been seen in the way that Twitter has had to try out different programs, regroup the way that it works and even ask people to try different things. While there are some opportunities for people to create sponsored advertisements on the site, it is not exactly the same caliber as Facebook or other social media sites.

Net Worth is Reflective

With a lower than average net worth for what would be expected of someone who has two successful businesses, Jack Dorsey has seen somewhat of a hardship especially when it comes to Twitter. He has a net worth of only 1.2 billion dollars and continues to collect a salary from both of the businesses that he runs. The net worth, though, is not all bad. It has continued to rise even when Twitter has taken hardships from different issues that they have had.

With the recent closure of Twitter's ever popular Vine service, it was expected that Dorsey's net worth would have decreased, but it continues to stay steady right around the 1 billion dollar mark. While Twitter has closed Vine, they are expected to roll out many new programs that will be able to change the way that people think about the social media site. They will be able to do more with the options that they have on Twitter.

Many are hopeful that Twitter will be able to grow to a point where it is optimized for earning but since that was never Dorsey's intention, it is unlikely that it will happen.

Will it Grow?

Only time will tell if Jack Dorsey's original social media baby will continue to grow in a world that is moving in a different direction. One thing is almost certain, though. Square is going to continue to grow and has the possibility of eventually replacing the traditional card reader systems that are seen around the world. While Dorsey may have struck out when it comes to social media with Twitter, he has been able to see a great deal of success with Square. Even if neither of the businesses works out, Jack Dorsey's entrepreneurial spirit is sure to allow him to keep pushing on and doing more while increasing the business opportunities that he has.

Chapter 5: Andrew Mason

With a site that is based on discounts of some of the hottest products, Andrew Mason has made a name for himself as a young entrepreneur. Clocking in at just under 40 years old, Mason was able to make a list as a young entrepreneur with the company that he founded, Groupon. He has been successful in the time that he has created the company but the true success lies in the actual business and the worth of it which is far more than his personal net worth.

Groupon Deals

The idea behind Groupon is that people will be able to get the deals that they want for services and products that are very popular. They are able to log onto the website and get a percentage off on products and services so that they are able to use them. This is a great way for people, especially families, to save money.

It is also a way for people who have businesses to get the most out of the advertising that the site offers. Without offering the percentage off of their services, small businesses like Sally's Nail Salon may never get a large number of customers that they currently do. They are able to create their own advertisements by offering their services while simultaneously building a repertoire with the people who are present in their business settings. The idea behind it is that they are going to be advertising their services, drawing in clients and still making money off of the clients. It is an opportunity that pays in the way that they are able to make money. It sends in more business than traditional advertising and also pays them back unlike traditional advertising.

Saying No to Partnerships

When Groupon was first started, it was a local thing only. It was Chicago-based, and it allowed people the chance to see that they could do much more with the money that they were spending on things. Andrew Mason wanted to make it about getting the best deals in Chicago, and he was successful with that. He eventually allowed it to include other areas around the United States and the world. Groupon is now able to offer people discounts on everything from activity trackers to 7-day vacations to European destinations. It has grown to be so much more than the original purpose behind it.

When Groupon was first getting started, the experts at Google saw that there was a lot of potential in the company. They offered an acquisition deal with the company which was somewhat of a lowball offer since Groupon was just getting started. Andrew Mason, with the help of others at Groupon, turned it down. The company is now flourishing and is worth much more than what the initial Google acquisition would have been worth to them.

Maturity Problems

The number one problem that came along with Groupon was the behavior of the CEO. He came from a somewhat humble upbringing in a suburb of Pittsburgh and became successful way too quickly. It was something that he could not handle, and it caused him to begin exhibiting reckless behavior. While the board of Groupon was able to deal with it and help to rope him back in for a short period of time, they eventually created a plan that would change his behavior and make him a better CEO.

Part of their plan involved phasing him out so that his poor behavior would not reflect the company as a whole and lowering the salary that they gave him so that he would not be able to continue the reckless antics that were a part of the problems he created for the company.

The plan failed, though and Andrew Mason was eventually relieved of his duties receiving around $350 which was only half of his yearly salary that would be included with the different things that he had associated with Groupon. It was a problem but something that Mason's entrepreneurial spirit would be able to overcome.

Lowered Net Worth

After he had been let go from his own company, Mason's net worth plummeted to around 200 million dollars which was not much for a 3 billion dollar company. He knew, though, that he had to do something different and that he had to be mature about it the second time around.

Mason is an entrepreneur, and he knew that his success got in the way of his drive in the past and he was determined not to let it happen again. He eventually married, found new opportunities and helped himself get out of the irresponsible behavior that he was exhibiting. This paid off for him and, even though he had severed ties with Groupon, he could still enjoy the success of the company once again.

New Opportunities

With Groupon out of the way when it came to being able to do more with companies and truly act as an entrepreneur, Mason was ready to get "back in the saddle." After he had begun learning new behavior models that were more akin to CEO and less to frat brother, he was able to begin working on new business opportunities. He learned from his mistakes and, like a true entrepreneur, turned them into a good thing. He is constantly looking forward to the next big opportunity.

Since he knew that he got successful too quickly with Groupon, he is taking it slow this time. Because of that, there is no word on what his next big thing will be, but it is expected to outgrow Groupon and be even better for both people and businesses. It may be a good idea to keep tabs on Andrew Mason and get an idea of what is going to happen in the future. He is going to have some great businesses make their way into the world of technology and is going to continue to see success. Groupon is not the end of the road for Mason.

Chapter 6: Blake Ross

Yet another Ivy League-er, Blake Ross is also another technology mogul who saw a lot of success at a young age. If you have ever opened up a browser that *isn't* Explorer or Chrome, the chances are that you have used one of Blake Ross's products. He was one of the co-creators of Firefox and continues to expand his reach into different areas despite the fact that he is truly all about technology (don't worry, his other surprising adventures *are* loosely related to technology).

Video Games and AOL

Like most people who came from the same generation as Blake Ross, his days were spent playing on AOL, chatting with friends and designing the perfect city on Sim City. All of these experiences, though, for Ross allowed him the chance to do things differently. Unlike the rest of people who left their Sim Cities in the background as they grew up, Ross allowed how to work as the inspiration for his career in the future. He was able to create video games based on what he learned with AOL and Sim City.

The first time that he created a video game was when he was 10. By the time that he got to Stanford University (often touted as the Ivy of the West Coast), he was a full-blown programmer and had more experience than some of the professors who were teaching classes to people who had programming majors. This was something that allowed him the chance to be extremely successful while he was in college and it gave him the chance to do more with the business that he had while he was also learning how to do other things.

Facebook and Netscape

After graduating college, he began to work with Netscape. This was a company that had the best technology of the time and allowed him to do much more than what he could do on his own. They used his experience as a programmer, and he used their resources as a springboard for his own success. He learned a lot about the programs and began working with another employee. They both eventually left Netscape to work on their own project – Firefox.

While working on the project, he still needed to have an actual job. During this time, he was hired as a developer at Facebook. This was still at the time that Facebook was just starting to take off and Ross was one of the reasons that it was able to take off in the way that it did. He did a lot of work on Facebook and helped to develop some of the programs that have allowed it to have continued success. Ross still has a working relationship with Zuckerberg and some of the other influencers at Facebook. He remains on good terms with them and even allowed his friendships to be the inspiration behind one of his later entrepreneurial ventures that he has had recently.

No Vision for the Past

One thing that Blake Ross recently found out about himself is that he is not able to visualize anything. For many entrepreneurs, the visualization of what they are going to do (or have done in the past) is the inspiration behind their respective journeys but for Ross is it just something that he cannot do. It would be similar to Zuck not being able to picture who is on his friend's list or you not being able to recall the visions that you saw while you were on your morning run today.

Blake Ross never even knew that he had this condition until recently. He had no idea that he was supposed to be able to pull up images of things that he wants to see or that he has seen in the past, so it has not really affected him. Some of the problems that can come along with the condition include anxiety, decreased motivation and problems with memory but Blake Ross has not had these as a result of the condition. Instead, he has been able to flourish with the different things that he does and that he can change the way that things are done.

Net Worth of Ross

Currently, Ross has a net worth of around 150 million dollars. It is something that fluctuates and depends on how well Firefox is doing on the market, but it has been steadily rising since he has taken on new opportunities and learned to do different things with the entrepreneurship attitude that he has about life. He has not stopped at Firefox, and he continues to do more with the different options that he has.

While he is a developer first and foremost, he also has interests that lie in different areas. He recognizes that he is great at the technology-based things that he does, but he also wants to make sure that he is able to do other things in addition to just providing technology. He does a lot of different things with the money that he has made, and this has allowed him to do more.

Writing Screenplays

It is not uncommon for young entrepreneurs, especially those who are all present around the same industry, to be friends with each other. Blake Ross, though, has taken the chance to cash in on the friendships that he has. He doesn't ask Brian Chesky for a free Airbnb or Zuck for free advertising on Facebook. Instead, he wrote a screenplay about his life as one of the elite members of the technology-driven entrepreneur club.

His screenplay is based on his friendships, technology, money and all of the fake (or maybe real) drama that he has experienced in Silicon Valley. The screenplay was picked up by HBO and has become a major hit by the same name of the area that so many of these people live, work and play. He is unique in that he has branched his entrepreneurial spirit into the world of the arts. He is the first to combine technology, making money and writing television shows.

Chapter 7: Jennifer Fleiss

If you haven't noticed already, the majority of entrepreneurs are Ivy

League graduates. This is not because they are smarter than

everyone, but they are the ones who work much harder at what they want to be able to do when they are working toward a goal. Jennifer Fleiss is no exception to the rule and began working hard from a young age so that she would be able to be successful at everything that she did. She isn't necessarily more talented, but she does have a drive that is far beyond what "normal" business people have.

Yale and Harvard

Jennifer Fleiss graduated at the top of her class from Yale University in 2005. Like many of her fellow graduates, she went on to graduate school. Instead of sticking with what she already knew, she decided to challenge herself and do something that she knew was going to be harder. She applied to the Harvard School of Business upon graduation and waited to hear if she got in.

Once she was accepted to the program, she worked hard and even graduated with her Master's earlier than what she had expected. She did this in a short time period so that she would not have to waste more time in school and so that she would be able to get further along in the career that she wanted to be able to have. She was a businesswoman, and she knew exactly what she wanted to do. She already had ideas in mind but knew that her education was the most important thing when it came to being successful so that she would be equipped with all of the tools that she needed to be able to have.

Rent the Runway

While she was growing up in New York City, Jennifer Fleiss saw hundreds of thousands of women who were dressed in runway attire. While she wasn't exactly destitute growing up, she knew that her parents would never be able to afford that type of clothing and that the chances were low that *she* would be able to afford it at any point during her life. For that reason, she wanted to make sure that the type of clothing was accessible to women at a reasonable price and without having to shop the boutiques that normally carried the runway looks.

This is how Rent the Runway was born. Jennifer Fleiss wanted to give women the chance to try these clothes out. They were either able to do it because they wanted to dress in high fashion styles or because they wanted to try something on before they dropped the thousands of dollars that it normally took to get a look like this. She made it all possible through Rent the Runway and allowed women the chance to do different things with their wardrobes.

The idea behind the business is that women can sign up for membership. They then choose outfits that they like and they can rent them and return them then get new ones in exchange for sending the old ones back. The rental service is based on key pieces and essentially works like a library, but instead of Walt Whitman and Jane Austen, women are able to check out Versace and Louis Vuitton. It is a great way for them to spend their money in a reasonable way and still get the looks that they love. And, in reality, who wears the same Chanel gown more than once in their life, anyway? It would be a travesty.

Awards for Business

Since the launch of Rent the Runway, Jennifer Fleiss and her co-founder (the other Jennifer) have been recognized for various awards. She was one of the top female entrepreneurs for several years in a row and even won the number one businesswoman spot in a category that she had never even dreamed of being a part of. Along with the female-specific awards that Jennifer has won, she has been able to compete with the "big dogs" in the world of technology and even retail. While she isn't exactly the same caliber as Wal-Mart, she has made a name for her niche business and others have even tried to copy her – one of the success indicators of a good entrepreneur.

Presentations about Success

Now that Rent the Runway has over 375 employees who are able to run the business successfully (many of them women who are empowered with a company that was based on helping other women and working together), Fleiss has been able to take a backseat to the micromanagement of the business. She still works toward the success of Rent the Runway, but she also works toward the success of other women.

She does talks and presentations about being an entrepreneur, business, and success that can come in many forms to help inspire women. She wants to make sure that they are able to get the most out of what she has to offer and she constantly works to make sure that they are getting that. Because of the way that Fleiss was able to grow her business, she is also able to help other women grow theirs. The majority of her talks are about being successful, but they are also about being able to be a successful woman in a male-dominated industry.

Worth of the Business

While Rent the Runway is worth about 116 million dollars, Fleiss is worth just under half of that. At 40 million dollars, she is one of the most expensive female entrepreneurs in the industry due in part to her company and the presentations that she does. It is nearly unheard of for a person to be worth as much as one-third of their company let alone sitting on the line of half of their company but Fleiss has been able to do it successfully. Her worth is expected to grow over the coming years and Rent the Runway branches out to other areas of fashion.

Chapter 8: Cameron Johnson

Unlike many of the entrepreneurs who are on this list, Cameron Johnson does not have a specific business that he is tied to. He is a rare, true entrepreneur in that he has many different talents and he uses them all to do different things that allow him the chance to make the most out of the situations that he is in. He recognizes what is popular, devises plans to cash in on that and builds a business to correspond with it. He has been featured in many publications and has been able to show off his success, but many people still don't know exactly what it is that he does.

The First Million

When Cameron Johnson was nine years old, he started to create things that he marketed to his friends and family. These were things like invitations to birthday parties, customized papers and even letters that he designed on his own. He used these to get started and actually made money off of them. He knew that this was something that he could do for a long time because that is what people wanted.

When he was 19, he officially made his first million dollars. He did this with e-commerce, invitations, and customized things. It allowed him the chance to try out different opportunities and to grow his business in new ways. He wanted to make sure that he was able to do much more than what he originally set out to do and this allowed him the chance to make sure that he was doing more with the money that he made. It also allowed him to increase the money that he was making and do even more than what he originally wanted to be able to do.

Oprah's Buddy

When he was a little older, he made an appearance on Oprah's Big Give. He competed for a spot to be able to be sponsored by Oprah because everyone knows that is what she likes to do – give away to people who don't have it but who are very deserving of it. When he did this, he was able to launch his business and make sure that his career was as successful as possible each time that he launched a new product.

While his having Oprah standing behind him wasn't exactly detrimental, he was able to do the majority of the work on his own. He wanted to make sure that he was getting the most out of the different options that were included with being an entrepreneur and he was able to do it each time that he tried something new. He went from making invitations to doing custom work for people who needed his help. He didn't exactly make a huge name for himself, but he gave himself the chance to do more than he had ever done before in any of the businesses that he was a part of.

Hosting Shows

Now that Johnson has been able to be successful, he has begun hosting his own television shows. While it does not give away quite as much money as what Oprah's Big Give did, it does allow him to give back to people who are starting in the same spot that he did when he was first getting started. He lets people compete for the chance to "Beat the Boss, " and they are able to win money. This has allowed him the chance to help others in the way that he was helped.

He wants to make sure that he makes a name for himself and that he remains relevant no matter what. This is one of the keys to being an entrepreneur, and it allows him to be among the most successful in the industry. He has jumped around a lot with the different things that he offers, but they have all been successful. Despite the fact that he is able to focus on one area more than others, he has seen a lot of success with different things. He knows that creating variety is a key to being successful when acting as an entrepreneur.

Technology-Based

While most of the things that Cameron Johnson has done have been only loosely related, they have nearly all been a major part of the technology sector. While he isn't exactly a developer like some of the other people on this list, he has been able to do more with the ideas that he has other than just promoting them on social media. He makes sure that he is able to include technological advances in each of the things that he offers and this gives him a chance to do more with the things that he has for everyone. It also allows him to be one of the best entrepreneurs.

Whether he has created eCards, fun memes or even advertisements, Cameron Johnson has done his best to stay relevant in the world of basic technology. He appeals to nearly everyone, and this has allowed him to make big money. Despite the fact that he does not have a single business but, instead, many different ones, he has been successful.

Johnson is different than other entrepreneurs in that his success comes from a variety of things instead of one single thing that could fail. He has many sources of success and streams of income.

The Worth of Ideas

All of the ideas that Johnson has put into play have been things that he has seen be successful in the past. He knows the trends, he works on them, and he creates ideas based on them. This has allowed him to be successful and has given him a chance at doing more with the business that he has. He wants to make sure that he can stay on top of everything and that often means that he can do it through technology and other things that are ideal for the help that he gets from other people.

Chapter 9: Alexa von Tobel

As a Morgan Stanley veteran and Harvard grad, Alexa von Tobel has been able to secure her spot in the male-dominated financial world as someone who puts the emphasis on women – who are quickly becoming the biggest group of people who are in the financial world and who are responsible for doing a lot of different things when it comes to both investing and the stock market. Alexa von Tobel created Learnvest, which is a company that teaches people *how* to invest and how to gets the most out of the investments that they make instead of just doing it for them in the way that investment companies did in the past.

The Experience

Alexa has experience in the financial industry in that she worked with Morgan Stanley and was one of the top people who worked for the company. She helped to make a lot of money for people who wanted to invest, and this was something that she saw as a way to help herself. While she was working there, she realized that she had a lot of skills when it came to investing and she wanted to be able to cash in on those for her own business.

Her entrepreneurial outlook on life led her to want to be able to work for herself and use those talents for her *own* benefits. She wanted to be able to get more out of the different things that were going on, and she didn't want to have to give up the money that she made and the ideas that she had for other people. While working, she also took her free time and dedicated it to raising money. She rose 25 million dollars as a way for her to get started with her own business and used it toward creating both a website and an app along with ways that she could market it to different people who needed her services.

For Women

While the app is available for anyone who wants to use it and learn how to invest, it is geared more toward women and people who have never had a chance to invest in the past. Alexa von Tobel recognized that there were not enough women in the industry and certainly not enough who were making what they could from investing. She wanted to change that and make it different. She wants women to be equally represented in the industry that has a lot of men. She knows, based on her own experience that women can often be even better at men when it comes to investing.

Everything that she does is about empowering women. Whether she is doing TED talks for women who want to be able to make more money, teaching them specifically on her app or showing them the right way to be able to do different things, Alexa knows that it is important that women have a chance to learn about investing so that they can be as successful as men when it comes to the investments that they make. She wants everyone to do their best and believes that empowering women is just one more step in the right direction for the financial world.

A Young Age

Looking past the fact that Alexa is a woman in a male-dominated field, it is also evident that she had to overcome other barriers that would have normally prevented someone from seeing the same type of success that she saw. Alexa is very young for the way that she does things, and she is one of the youngest investors that Morgan Stanley ever saw. This is something that sets her apart from others who are on this list. She finished school and started her own business at such a young age and was able to use that to her own advantage while she was working for herself.

Now that she is older, she is seeing people who are the same age as her just getting a taste of the success that she saw in her early twenties. As one of the youngest investors and business owners, she stands far above others who are just getting started with their successful entrepreneurship.

Subscription Service

Apart from being a service that is dedicated to helping women invest, Learnvest is also one of the first of its kind that allows people to have a subscription to learn how to invest. This is something that Alexa can take advantage of and something that she has been able to do her best with. She knows that it is a good way for her to do different things and it has allowed her the chance to do more. While other businesses have completed, none of them are able to do as much as what she has done with her business.

Even though she is the first and has had some competition in the past, she still continues to have her business at the top of most lists. Alexa von Tobel wants to make sure that Learnvest is doing its best and she uses her own financial expertise to provide that to the company. She works as both the founder and the CEO of the company while she continues to be very hands-on about it which allows her the chance to do much more than other founders with their respective companies.

Invest in Worth

Since Learnvest has been on the market and has been helping women increase their net worth, Alexa von Tobel's *own* net worth has actually increased at the time that she has been doing things with the business. This is one of the indicators of her success as an entrepreneur and shows that she is going to continue to be successful. While her net worth sits around 100 million dollars, she is expected to be worth much more especially with new investment options that are being rolled out in the app for other people who want to enjoy them when they are using Learnvest.

Chapter 10: How You Can Be Successful, Too

After reading about how people are less than 40 years old and worth into the billions of dollars, you may be asking yourself how that is going to help you. Even if you are 26 years old, making 15 dollars per hour at a car dealership with your community college associates degree in business, you can *still* be just as successful as the people who are on the list. The thing about these young entrepreneurs is just that...they are young. They are, in fact, still much younger than the age that most people are just getting started in their career as an entrepreneur. It doesn't take making a million dollars at 19, graduating from an Ivy or even knowing the right people. What it *does* take is outlined below.

Inspiration

Every single one of the people who is listed in this book has something in common (actually, they have a lot of things in common). They all had inspiration. Whether they were inspired by their college friends connecting on a chatroom, couture fashion on the streets of New York or Sim City, they had the inspiration that they knew they needed to be able to get where they wanted to in life.

Instead of looking at something and longing for it in the way that most people did, they looked at something and tried to figure out *how* they were going to get it. They were inspired by things, made a plan for getting those things and ran with it so that they would be able to do more with it. This allowed them the chance to do more with their entrepreneurial attitudes and gave them a chance to truly be successful while they were working toward different things.

No matter where your inspiration lies, don't just think about it. Do something about the things that you want.

Hard Work

Most of the people who are on this list worked very hard to get there. They were not handed opportunities by their parents or anyone else, and they were certainly not able to do different things because they were given the opportunity to do them. They worked hard. Whether that meant that they worked hard on their grades to get into the best school, they worked to grow their business to new levels, or they worked to make it successful and make the kind of money that they wanted, each entrepreneur was able to focus on the hard work that they could do to be able to provide more opportunities for themselves.

The hard work is something that may take some work on your part. Maybe you need to work hard to raise money to be able to start your business, or maybe you need to work hard when it comes to marketing yourself and telling people about the business that you have. No matter what you need to do to become an entrepreneur, know that it is going to be hard work and that you are going to have to work at it.

When you are successful and worth much more than you had ever dreamed of, you will be able to look back on the hard work that you did and see that it all paid off in the end.

Motivation

Always stay motivated. No matter what you are doing, you are going to need the motivation to be able to get there. You should make sure that you are motivating yourself and that it does not come from an outside source because the chances are that the source could change at any point in time, but you will always be stuck with yourself when you are doing different things so do your best to be able to use that to your advantage.

Even if you use something as your inspiration, you should always be your own motivation. Stay motivated. Try to remember what you are doing this for, how successful you want to be and who you are doing it for. The answer to that should be yourself and to have the things that you want. Success is great, and it can be your motivation for continuing on each of the hard journeys toward the entrepreneur like things that you want to do.

Waking Up

One thing that most successful people do that others do not is that they wake up one hour earlier than they need to. It is like adding an extra hour to their day, and it allows them to get things done. Whether they take that time to exercise, meditate or even prepare for their day, they are all doing something productive during that time. It allows them the chance to make sure that they are getting the most out of their days and that they will be able to be successful no matter what they are trying to do.

If you are able to wake yourself up one hour earlier every day, you should see your productivity increase by leaps and bounds. You will likely not even miss the sleep that you could have been getting in the morning because you will be doing so well at all of the extra things that you have done. It will allow you the chance to make sure that you are getting the most out of your day and it will truly feel like you have added an extra hour onto the day. It will also allow you the chance to do more with what you have, and you may even get more done throughout the rest of the day.

Nonchalance

You may be surprised to find that many entrepreneurs have a very nonchalant attitude. This is not to say that they don't care about what they are doing or the success that they are going to have in the future, but they do not really care about what is going on with the different issues that they come across. They don't let small failures (or even very big ones) have an effect on them.

You can take on this type of attitude by just brushing yourself off each time that you come across a situation that is trying or troublesome. You will want to make sure that you are always thinking about success and this will help to keep you from letting failures have a huge negative effect on yourself. It will also give you a chance to make sure that you are getting the most out of the different ideas of your success. Be nonchalant like an entrepreneur, and you will be successful in no time.

Chapter 11: Bonus Content – Entrepreneur Checklist

No matter what type of entrepreneur you want to be or what type of business you want to run, you will need some basic things. These are all actual material things as well as ideologies that will help you to become better at what you do. Use this list to help get you as successful as possible and to keep you from having problems when it comes to being an entrepreneur. There are even spaces provided for you to add your *own* ideas to the list that will pertain to your specific business and the way that you want your entrepreneurial lifestyle to work for you.

Attitude

- ☐ Positive outlook
- ☐ Inspiration found somewhere
- ☐ Ideas about success
- ☐ Motivation in the form of self
- ☐ People to look up to
- ☐ People who will be able to support you
- ☐ Clear vision of what success will look like
- ☐ Organization that will allow for optimal success
- ☐ Dedicated time to be able to work
- ☐ Space where you can dream about success
- ☐ Practice with being more extroverted
- ☐ Ability to look past problems (practice!)
- ☐ Understanding there will be problems
- ☐ _____
- ☐ _____
- ☐ _____

Behaviors

- ☐ Wake up one hour earlier
- ☐ Pick up a productive habit

- ☐ Do more each day
- ☐ Create lists that will help you decide what you need to do
- ☐ Prioritize different things that are on your list
- ☐ Try new time management skills
- ☐ Do more with the ideas that you have
- ☐ Create a dream board including your goals
- ☐ Let people know you want to be an entrepreneur
- ☐ Do one thing each day that scares you
- ☐ Take on more – do not stress over things that you need to get done
- ☐ Make extra time for yourself – exercise, meditation, etc.
- ☐ Stop the bad habits now
- ☐ Be friendly
- ☐ _____
- ☐ _____
- ☐ _____

Capital

- ☐ Save as much money as you comfortably can
- ☐ Cut out your morning cup of coffee – save that money
- ☐ Use cash, it is cheaper
- ☐ Minimize your debt obligations

Young Entrepreneurs

- ☐ Pay off anything that you can start with the largest ones first
- ☐ Consider making smart investments with your savings
- ☐ If you can't invest, find a high-interest savings account
- ☐ Avoid gimmicky offers
- ☐ Put your money where you know it will be safe and grow
- ☐ Cut down on some of the expenses (buy secondhand, make lunch at home, drink water instead of wine)
- ☐ _____
- ☐ _____
- ☐ _____

Contacts

- ☐ Say hello to every person you meet
- ☐ Keep in contact with people you meet at work
- ☐ Go to mixers
- ☐ Go to upscale places
- ☐ Avoid seedy bars and places in town that could be harmful to you
- ☐ Don't gossip (about friends, coworkers or people on the street)
- ☐ Keep in touch with your family
- ☐ Let everyone you meet know what you are trying to do

☐ Attend events related to your business

☐ Do the best work possible at your current job

☐ Don't quit until you're a successful entrepreneur

☐ _____

☐ _____

☐ _____

Marketing

☐ Consider alternative marketing (online, etc.)

☐ Talk to marketing agencies

☐ Try something new with marketing

☐ Market yourself – continue telling people who you are and what you want to do

☐ Let your friends know what you're doing – they could market you

☐ Make contacts in marketing but *don't* ask for a discount (if they like you, they'll give you one without asking)

☐ Create ads that *you* like as a consumer instead of basing them on trends

☐ Take advantage of your

☐ personal social media and use that as free marketing opportunities

Young Entrepreneurs

- ☐ _____
- ☐ _____
- ☐ _____

Earnings

- ☐ Be smart about the money that you make
- ☐ Invest 50% of *profit* back into the business
- ☐ Save as much as you can
- ☐ Don't invest your entrepreneur money unless it is 100% safe (no investment is 100% so just don't do it)
- ☐ Get a business bank account
- ☐ Try to avoid loans and, instead, use the money that you saved up at the beginning
- ☐ Don't get sucked into gimmicks
- ☐ Only hire out when you need to
- ☐ Do as much work on your own as you can – some entrepreneurs work up to 20 hours per day, but it is worth it for them
- ☐ There's always a chance to make more money – take it!
- ☐ _____
- ☐ _____
- ☐ _____

There are so many entrepreneurs who do not have the same opportunities as the people who have come before them. With technology helping to keep the world running, you have more chances than ever at getting what you want when it comes to being an entrepreneur. Take these opportunities and run with them. Cash in on them while you can.

Use the people who are included in this book as your inspiration to do more, use the information contained in the chapters for ideas on how you can be successful and, by all means, use the checklist to your own advantage to make sure that you include all of the information that is in the book and to be as successful as possible. Just make sure that you are doing this for yourself and so that you can have more money. Try your hardest to do everything that you can for you and for nobody else. It will be easier to stay motivated if you are doing it on your own than if you are doing it for your family, friends or someone else who is in your life.

The best part about being an entrepreneur is doing things on your own terms and making money that way. Take that, run with it and have fun doing it. This will give you a chance to do more than what you were intending to do and will allow you to be as successful as possible. Having money is fun but being your own boss while you are successful is even better than having to work for someone else for the rest of your life.

Conclusion

Thank for making it through to the end of this book, let's hope it was informative and able to provide you with all of the tools you need to achieve your goals whatever they may be.

The next step is to start saving your money to begin your entrepreneurship. After that, the world is yours, and you will be able to do everything that you can to make sure that you are getting the most out of what you can do with your own money and your own business opportunities. Take it the way that you want it and provide yourself with the best opportunities possible.

Finally, if you found this book useful in any way, a review on Amazon is always appreciated!